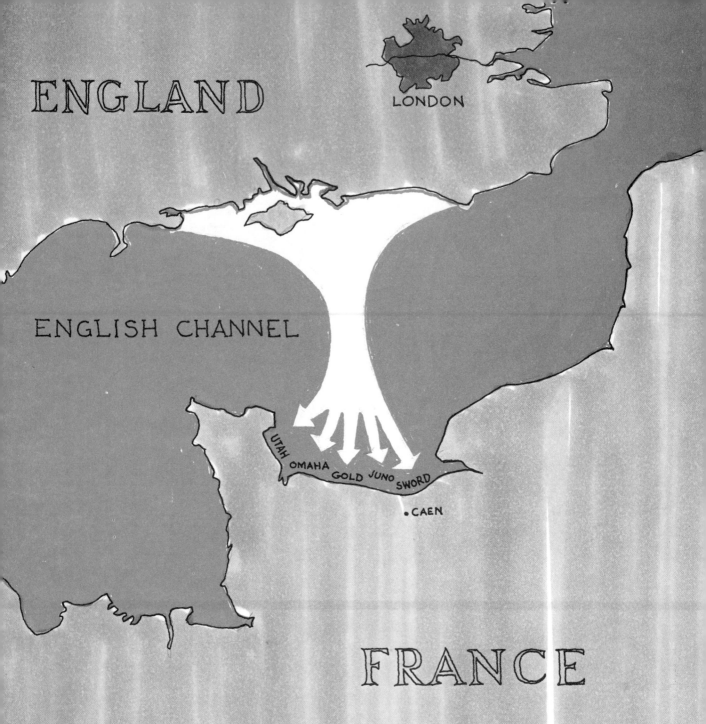

Cornerstones of Freedom

The Story of
D-DAY

By R. Conrad Stein

Illustrated by Tom Dunnington

CHILDRENS PRESS, CHICAGO

Library of Congress Cataloging in Publication Data

Stein, R   Conrad.
  The story of D-Day.

  (Cornerstones of freedom)
  SUMMARY: Describes the events of the Allied landing
on the beaches of Normandy, June 6, 1944, the largest
invasion ever attempted in history.
  1. World War, 1939-1945—Campaigns—France—Normandy
—Juvenile literature. 2. Normandy—History—Juvenile
literature. [1. World War, 1939-1945—Campaigns—France
—Normandy. 2. Normandy—History] I. Dunnington, Tom.
II. Title.
D756.5.N6S73   940.54'21   77-5089
ISBN 0-516-04609-8

The engines from large aircraft roared above the town of Caen in France on the night of June 5, 1944. The people of Caen thought another group of bombers was passing over their town. One man, a veteran of the French army, looked up at the planes in the moonlit night. He saw a line of six two-engined planes, each one followed closely by six peculiar-looking aircraft that had no propellers. As two of the planes came nearer, the man thought he saw a cable connecting one of the two-engined planes to one of the propellerless planes. Those aren't bombers, the Frenchman thought to himself. They're gliders.

The planes and the gliders rumbled over Caen, and disappeared into the night. Thirty men and hundreds of pounds of equipment were jammed into each glider. Their destination was a region called Normandy in the coastal section of France. Two important bridges there were held and guarded by German troops. The Allies needed those bridges. The men in the gliders were British paratroopers who had trained for months to perform this one operation.

At a precise moment, the towing cables were released and the planes roared into the clouds while the gliders whispered down toward the earth. Looking like huge black eagles, the gliders swooped down toward the two bridges that could just barely be seen in the light of a full moon. As their crafts inched toward the ground, the glider pilots tried to pick out smooth areas where they could land close to the bridges, yet bring them down as gently as possible.

One pilot thought he had found a good spot in a cornfield near the river. He eased his craft down and waited, hoping for a soft landing. With a crash and a jerk the undercarriage of the glider hit the cornfield and bounced upward. The glider hit the ground again and skidded across the field as if it were plowing a fresh row of corn. Finally the glider came to the end of its long skid and settled in the dirt of the cornfield. There was a second of almost churchlike silence.

"All right, lads, let's go," said an officer.

The men clambered out of the glider and rushed the bridge. The rattle of a machine gun broke the silence. Then grenades exploded, and

hundreds of tracer bullets with bright red trails
streaked into the night. The Germans defending
the bridges were shocked by the surprise attack,
and the well-trained British paratroopers
pressed toward their objective. The British over-
whelmed German foxholes, one after another,
with grenades, rifle fire, and bayonets. Soon
paratroopers charged over the bridge and at-
tacked German positions on the far side of the
river.

In only fifteen minutes the first battle of D-Day was over. The bridge had been captured and the British were rounding up German prisoners. One young paratrooper felt strangely disappointed. He had practiced this operation for months, and now that it was all over it seemed to have been ridiculously easy.

Other battles fought during this first day of the huge Allied invasion of Europe would not be so easy.

In England, American General Eisenhower paced the floor of the house trailer he used as an office. Hours earlier he had wrestled with the decision to postpone the invasion. A storm raged at sea, and the thousands of troops jammed in the flat-bottomed landing boats were bouncing about in the waters off France, most of them hopelessly seasick. A new weather front moving from the south promised calm seas for the sixth of June, but after that the weather would deteriorate again. Eisenhower would have but one day to launch the most massive invasion attempt in history.

If the invasion were to be postponed, it would be almost a full month before there would again be enough moonlight for the airborne troops. The thousands of men assembled for D-Day could not be cooped up that long, and the American general feared someone would talk and the Germans would learn of the coming invasion. "I don't like it," he told a group of officers on the afternoon of June 5. "I don't like it, but we're stuck with it. D-Day will be the sixth of June."

In a small town in Germany, far away from the invasion beaches, Field Marshal Erwin Rommel drank coffee in his home. More than a year earlier he had been chosen by Adolf Hitler to construct defenses in France and to command the German troops who would oppose an Allied invasion of Europe. Rommel was a hero in Germany, and he was respected by all of the Allied generals. At the start of the war he earned the title "The Desert Fox" by skillfully maneuvering his tank divisions in North Africa to win battle after battle against the British. But by 1944 Rommel and the German armies were on the defensive. Allied forces in Italy were steadily pushing the Germans backward, and in the east the mighty Russian army rolled toward the German border.

Rommel knew he could expect an Allied invasion any day in northern France. For months he had feverishly supervised the construction of enormous concrete bunkers that were armed with artillery and machine guns. Miles and miles of barbed wire were strung out on the beaches, mines were buried in the sand, and steel posts designed to rip open the bottoms of landing boats were embedded in the sand just below the water level.

The field marshal hoped to turn the shoreline of northern Europe into one vast fortress that the Allies would never dare invade. But there were many miles of beaches, and not enough time. The great Atlantic wall Rommel hoped to create was strong in some places, but weak in others. And Rommel had no idea when or where the Allies would strike.

For the moment, Rommel felt at peace and was enjoying his vacation at home. Weather reports told him that a storm was lashing the

beaches on both sides of the English Channel, and he was sure the Allies would never land in such conditions. Besides, June 6 was his wife's birthday, and he wanted to spend the day with his family.

At midnight, June 5, airplanes flying low and fast raced over the beaches at Normandy. In the darkness, German anti-aircraft gunners thought they were fighters. Searchlights flicked on and German guns poured shell after shell at the formation. The planes weaved between the shell bursts and tried to dodge the long fingers of searchlight beams.

The aircraft the Germans fired at were Dakota transport planes, each of them packed with paratroopers. These first American paratroopers to drop on France were a small group of specially trained volunteers called "pathfinders." They were to land, move into predetermined positions, and mark drop zones with lights and flares. They would be followed by thousands of paratroopers from the 82nd and 101st Airborne Divisions.

The carefully thought out Allied invasion plans ran into difficulties from the beginning. The unexpectedly heavy anti-aircraft barrage forced many of the Dakota transports off course. Of the 120 pathfinders who jumped during the early hours of June 6, fewer than 40 landed near their target. The others were scattered over the French countryside—many miles away from their appointed areas.

It did not take long for one veteran pathfinder to realize he had been dropped at the wrong spot. He crouched in a ditch studying his map with a small penlight. None of the terrain around him looked remotely like what was shown on the map. He snapped off his penlight and folded up his map. The flares he carried that were supposed to mark a drop zone were useless now. He thought about his paratrooper comrades who would be jumping within an hour. "Those poor guys," he whispered. "They're going to have to come in blind."

The roar of a huge formation of airplanes flying over the English Channel was deafening. Even veteran German soldiers held their hands over their ears to protect their eardrums. Almost nine hundred planes raced over Normandy; they were about to drop thirteen

thousand paratroopers in what would be the
largest airborne assault ever attempted.

The paratroopers were to land in a long
narrow area behind the main landing beaches.
There they would dig in and try to prevent German counterattacks on the main forces that
would hit the beaches at sunrise. As the planes
moved toward the landing zones, paratroop
commanders searched the ground for signals
from their pathfinders. Finding no signals, the
commanders relied on their navigation and gave
the order to jump.

Looking like falling sticks, men tumbled out
of the hundreds of airplanes. When their
parachutes opened, the thousands of men looked
like the contents of a bag of confetti that had
been emptied from a roof. After the roar of
planes faded away, many of the men floating to
earth thought they heard the distant chiming of
church bells. For some it would be the last sound
they would ever hear.

Most of the paratroopers dropped safely to
the ground in flat fields. Many landed with their
chutes hung up on trees and had to cut them-

selves down. Others landed in swamps created by Rommel, who had flooded fields to prevent airborne attack. Those who could not free themselves from their hundred-pound packs drowned, sometimes in water less than two feet deep. At least one planeload of paratroopers jumped directly into the North Atlantic, where all disappeared in the black water.

There were other tragic errors committed during the early morning hours of D-Day.

A fire raged in a house in the Normandy village of Ste.-Mère-Eglise. The bell of the tall church that stood in the village square chimed wildly to summon firefighters. Townspeople formed a bucket brigade and passed water from a well to the burning house. The people of the village worked under the watchful eyes of German soldiers.

Suddenly a German soldier shouted, *"Fallschirmjäger! Fallschirmjäger!"* (Paratroopers! Paratroopers!) Everyone looked toward the sky, bright from the light of the burning house. Dozens of men, dangling from parachutes, were floating helplessly into the town.

Those airborne soldiers were supposed to have dropped into a field south of the town, but pilot error and high winds had thrown them off course. The Germans opened fire with machine guns and rifles. Many Americans were killed before their feet ever touched French soil. Others crashed into houses or into the square itself, where they were either killed or taken prisoner.

General Eisenhower sat in his office smoking cigarette after cigarette. Initial reports from the airborne divisions told of confusion and heavy casualties. What would happen at sunrise, he thought, when the main invasion forces hit the beach?

Five hundred miles away from Normandy, Field Marshal Rommel slept soundly. German officers at the front heard word of an airborne assault, but the reports were sketchy and communication was difficult. The French underground had been cutting telephone wires again, and the airways were being jammed by American transmissions. One high-ranking German officer assumed the reports of parachute landings at Normandy meant merely that crew members of a bomber had bailed out of a damaged plane. Anyway, the German officer thought, the landing of a few paratroopers was no reason to disturb General Rommel on his vacation.

It was still dark at 5:00 A.M. when a midget submarine splashed to the surface in the waters a mile from a beach at Normandy. The submarine crew numbered only five men, but the sub was so small that each crew member felt cramped. This British submarine, the X-20, had been hiding below the surface for two days. Twenty miles away another midget submarine, the X-23, also popped to the surface. These two subs marked the boundaries of the British and Canadian beaches. On D-Day morning they would stand like goal posts on a football field, guides for hundreds of landing craft carrying thousands of soldiers.

The five crew members of the X-20 climbed to the deck of their tiny craft and began erecting a mast. On top of the mast they would attach a flashing green light and a large yellow flag. These markers could be seen for miles, and would guide the landing craft to the correct beach. But, as every crew member knew, they would also make perfect targets for German artillery.

Behind the two midget subs was the most incredible armada ever assembled. Battleships, cruisers, destroyers, and frigates eased toward Normandy. Landing craft of every size and description tossed about in the choppy seas like toy boats in a bathtub. Not even Allied commanders knew exactly how many ships were assembled for D-Day, but the closest guess was four thousand. There were enough sailors manning boats and soldiers waiting to land to populate a small city.

The sea was calmer now, but the flat-bottomed landing craft still bounced with every wave. Seasickness from the night before had caused even the strongest men to cry without shame. Decks were slick with vomit, and during the night some of the men had felt so miserable they had to be held back from jumping overboard. Many of the soldiers packed into landing craft did not care how many machine guns the

Germans had on the beaches. They wanted only to put their feet on solid ground.

Most of the German soldiers on the Normandy beaches were asleep in their bunkers as the sun inched upward. One young German soldier on watch yawned and looked out to sea. As on most mornings, a fog obscured his view of the horizon. He looked back to land and like all soldiers standing guard duty, was soon lost in a daydream. Fifteen minutes passed, and the German looked out to sea again. He could scarcely believe what he saw. Dotting the water were ships with guns that all seemed to be pointing directly at him. He tried to count them, but it seemed that with every passing second another dozen warships popped out of the fog. This was the invasion. He was sure of it. The Allies would strike this morning.

There was a thunderous roar as the big ships opened fire. Huge battleship guns fired fourteen-inch shells. Smaller shells barked out of the destroyers. German troops hiding in concrete bunkers pressed their hands over their ears and felt themselves bouncing about as if the entire earth was shaking. When the shelling lifted, German soldiers heard the roar of airplane engines and braced themselves for a bombing attack.

Planes dropping bombs covered the sky like a steel umbrella. Young Allied troops watching the bombardment from landing craft were certain that no one could live through this holocaust. It seemed that the entire beach was exploding. But the veterans knew better. There would still be plenty of Germans left when they landed.

Long lines of assault craft churned toward
shore. Each one of the American, British,
Canadian, and Free French soldiers crowded
into the boats felt alone with his fears. Would
the beaches be mined? Would the Germans use
poison gas?

Boats carrying American soldiers of the 29th
Division moved toward a beach that had the
code name "Omaha." Peering over the tops of
the ramps, the soldiers saw Rommel's han-
diwork. Concrete and steel posts jutted from the
sand of the beach. The tops of the posts were

mined, and barbed wire was strung between them. The beach looked like a steel jungle.

The clumsy landing boats bounced in the waves as they bored toward the beach. Four hundred yards to go, now three hundred. Where were the Germans? Would this be an easy landing? Suddenly one of the landing craft exploded. Shattered bodies flew from it and splashed into the water. Another landing craft was hit and sank like a rock.

The German artillery pieces that were dug into the cliffs near Omaha looked directly down on the long lines of slow-moving boats. "This will be like target practice," one German soldier said to his sergeant.

Still the hundreds of landing boats moved forward. They bumped against the beach, ramps dropped, and men laden with heavy packs splashed into water that was anywhere from three to six feet deep. German machine guns opened fire at the men wading through the water. History would remember this beachhead as "bloody Omaha."

On another American beach, code named Utah, General Theodore Roosevelt studied a map. His men of the 4th Division, unlike those who had landed at nearby Omaha Beach, had had only a few shots fired at them. The general looked confused as he stared at the map. Finally he called a major over to him and said, "We're on the wrong beach."

The major read the map and agreed. Smoke created by the pre-invasion bombardment must have confused the pilots of the landing boats, and the 4th Division had hit the beach more than a mile away from their target. Thousands of troops were yet to land, and the major asked if they should land at the original site.

"Nope, our war starts right here," the general said as he pointed to the beach now held by the 4th Division. "Now let's move inland."

General Roosevelt would later learn how fortunate he and his men were to have landed at the wrong beach. The original landing site was defended by hundreds of Germans, all well dug in and heavily armed. Had the landing party hit the correct beach, the 4th Division would have faced the same slaughter as the men of the 29th were experiencing at Omaha.

The second wave of landing boats pushed to the sands of Omaha Beach. The GIs charging off the landing craft could hardly believe what they saw around them. Wrecked landing boats lay strewn on the beaches. Torn and bloody bodies were everywhere. Men hid behind anti-tank obstacles set up by the enemy while the Germans rained fire at them with machine guns, artillery, and mortars. New soldiers at Omaha became instant veterans as they plunged into the middle of this bloody battle.

As the GIs pressed themselves into the sand they were amazed to see one man calmly walking about the beach as if he were a civilian on his way to work. Colonel George Taylor of the 1st Infantry Division knew that courage is often born from necessity. He had put his life in the hands of fate and urged his men to do the same. The colonel walked erect, ignoring the furious German machine-gun fire. "Listen to me, men," he shouted above the din of battle. "There are only two kinds of men on this beach. Those who are already dead, and those who are about to die. Now let's go inland and die. Get off this damn beach."

One by one the American GIs got to their feet and advanced to the high ground in front of them. Many were cut down by machine-gun fire and still others were blown apart by mines, but the rest continued to push forward. By dusk of D-Day the Americans at Omaha had moved more than a mile inland. There had been twenty-five hundred casualties.

On Utah Beach, huge landing ships, their front hatches yawning open, pushed against the

beach while trucks, jeeps, tanks, and guns rolled
out of them. The scene reminded some of a
grotesque big-city traffic jam. Ahead, the front-
line troops of the 4th Division advanced at a
faster speed than anyone could have imagined.

The lead man of a 4th Division patrol walked
cautiously up a Normandy path. So far the GI
had seen no Germans. He turned a corner near a
patch of tall bushes. Suddenly he saw another
soldier and dove to the ground. The other man
saw the American and also hit the dirt. But both
recognized that the uniforms of their opponents
were not German.

The 4th Division GI hid behind a rock and
called out, "Hey, are you airborne?"

"Yeah," the paratrooper answered. "What
took you guys so long to get here?"

The midget submarines, X-20 and X-23, tore off their huge yellow flags and flashing green lights and set a course for England. They had marked the beaches for the thousands of British and Canadian soldiers who, like the Americans, were now fighting their way inland. All morning the Germans had shelled landing craft and any other ship that came within their range. But these two tiny submarines floating in the waves just a mile off shore escaped untouched. Now they could go home. Their job on D-Day was finished.

In his office in England, General Eisenhower smiled when he was told of the linkup between the airborne forces and the 4th Division at Utah Beach. He was sure he had a secure beachhead and wondered how soon he could go to France to congratulate his men.

It was just after ten in the morning in Germany when Field Marshal Rommel answered his phone. An excited German officer told him the Allies were landing a huge force at Normandy. Rommel listened quietly, and after he hung up, said, "Normandy. I should have known."

D-Day was over. The largest invasion ever attempted in history was a success. By nightfall, 155,000 Allied soldiers had landed at Normandy and had liberated eighty miles of French soil. In the months to come, the Allies would sweep toward Germany with such power that no one would be able to stop them.

Four months after D-Day, German Field Marshal Rommel was dead. He had been forced to take poison after he participated in a plot to assasinate Adolf Hitler, the man who had brought so much misery to Europe and the rest of the world. General Eisenhower retired from the army shortly after World War II. He later became the President of the United States.

On the Normandy beaches today there are many plaques and markers indicating sites of individual action that took place during this historic battle. Perhaps the most bittersweet of them all is a simple wooden sign that stands near the cliffs of Pointe du Hoc, where a brief but violent battle was fought. The sign reads:

HERE THE WARRIORS SLEEP. THE CHAOS OF
BATTLE HAS UNITED THEM FOR ETERNITY.

About the Author

R. Conrad Stein was born and grew up in Chicago. After serving a three-year enlistment in the Marine Corps, he attended the University of Illinois, and graduated with a Bachelor's Degree in history. He later studied in Mexico, and earned a more advanced degree.

The study of history is Mr. Stein's hobby, and he enjoys visiting historical sites. He once toured Europe and is familiar with Normandy and its beaches. He now lives in Mexico where he teaches creative writing and juvenile literature at the Instituto Allende in the town of San Miguel de Allende. Mr. Stein is the author of many other books, articles, and short stories written for young people.

About the Artist

Tom Dunnington divides his time between book illustration and wildlife painting. He has done many books for Childrens Press, as well as working on textbooks, and is a regular contributor to *Highlights for Children*. Tom lives in Elmhurst.